My Pet Lizards

My Pet Lizards

by **LeeAnne Engfer**
photographs by **Andy King**

Lerner Publications Company • Minneapolis

To Dave—L.E.

Acknowledgments
Thank you to Jamal, Jahan, Jaleh, Ali, and Taryn
Galehdari, who were interviewed and photographed for
this book. Thanks also to Tropical Concepts, Columbia
Heights, Minnesota; and to James E. Gerholdt, The
Remarkable Reptiles.

Additional photographs are reproduced with permission of the following
sources: © James E. Gerholdt, p. 10; Jim Simondet/Independent Picture
Service, pp. 24 (top), 33 (middle, right, and bottom); © Dwight R. Kuhn,
p. 33 (top), 40, 55 (all); © Walt Anderson, p. 49 (top); © Wolfgang
Kaehler, pp. 45 (both), 49 (middle left and right, lower left and right).

Website address: www.lernerbooks.com

Library of Congress Cataloging-in-Publication Data

Engfer, LeeAnne, 1963–
    My pet lizards / by LeeAnne Engfer ; photographs by Andy King.
      p.   cm. — (All about pets)
    Includes bibliographical references (p.   ) and index.
    Summary: Text and photographs follow eleven–year-old Jamal as he
  explains how he cares for his bearded dragon lizards and chameleons.
    ISBN 0-8225-2263-2
    1. Lizards as pets—Juvenile literature. 2. Chameleons as pets—
  Juvenile literature. [1. Lizards as pets. 2. Chameleons as pets. 3. Pets.]
  I. King, Andy, ill. II. Title. III. Series
    SF459.L5E53   1999
    639.3'95—dc21   98–2871

Manufactured in the United States of America
1 2 3 4 5 6 – JR – 04 03 02 01 00 99

Contents

CHAPTER 1 My family is crazy about pets 7

CHAPTER 2 Lizards must have heat and light 18

CHAPTER 3 Taking care of lizards is easy 29

CHAPTER 4 Eggie doesn't like to be ignored 37

CHAPTER 5 Chameleons have many moods 44

CHAPTER 6 I plan to have lizards for a long time 54

Glossary 60

Resources 61

For Further Reading 62

Index 63

My family is crazy about pets...

Everyone at school knows my family. We're the "pet family." My name is Jamal, and I'm in fifth grade. I have a brother, Jahan, who is 13, and a sister, Jaleh. She's nine. At our house we have a dog, lots of birds, fish, a rabbit, three chameleons, a turtle, a hamster, a snake, and two bearded dragon lizards. My pets are the bearded dragons, the turtle, and the hamster. I caught the turtle at Shingle Creek, near my house. Jahan, Jaleh, and I each have one chameleon.

My favorite pets are my bearded dragons.

The snake is Jaleh's— she says it's her best friend. Dad teaches our birds to talk.

When you walk into our house, it sounds kind of like a zoo. You hear the birds squawking or screeching and the dog barking. There's always a lot of activity. I think it's fun! My friends who don't have pets love coming to our house.

We have always had animals. My dad works at a pet store, and he raises birds at home. Some of our birds are Sugar, Apple, Cocoa, Beaker, Candy, Valentine, and Alligator. Alligator talks. He says, "I can talk. Can you fly?" and "Here, kitty, kitty." He meows like a cat, too.

Sometimes my dad brings our pets to my school for presentations. Not long ago, he brought my bearded dragons and one of the chameleons. I showed everyone in my class how the bearded dragons sit on my shoulders. Then they climbed onto my head. One dragon's tail slid against the edge of my nose. It tickled! Everybody cracked up.

Some of the kids in my class were afraid of the lizards. They wanted to know if they would bite. I said no. Other kids wanted to touch them.

Some lizards are friendly, and they like to be petted. Lizard skin feels cool. It is dry, not slimy.

I got my first lizard about a year ago. One day my dad came home from the pet store and told me they had a bearded dragon. "What's that?" I asked. Right away I liked the name—bearded dragon. It sounded like something from a fairy tale. Dad told me it was a lizard with a beard and spikes all over its body. He took me to the store to see it. I was pretty excited.

The bearded dragon was a baby, about 4 inches long. He was a light greenish brown color, with jagged stripes on his back. Horny scales covered his back and head. They felt like the teeth of a plastic comb. The "beard" is a throat pouch of loose skin. Lizards can flare out their beards to make themselves look tough.

A baby bearded dragon doesn't have much of a beard yet. Its throat pouch grows bigger as the lizard grows.

Scientific Names

Many lizards have a common name, such as bearded dragons or leopard geckos. All lizards also have a scientific name. If you are thinking about getting a lizard, it's helpful to know something about scientific names. Many guidebooks use them.

Scientists classify, or arrange, animals and plants into groups based on how similar or different they are. A large group of animals or plants is called a class. This group is divided into smaller and smaller groups that are more and more alike. The smallest group is called a species. Animals that belong to the same species are basically the same.

The scientific name of the inland bearded dragon is *Pogona vitticeps*. Here is a chart showing how the inland bearded dragon is classified:

CLASS	Reptilia	all reptiles
ORDER	Squamata	lizards and snakes
SUBORDER	Lacertilia or Sauria	lizards
FAMILY	Agamidae	agamids (a group of insect-eating lizards with similar teeth)
GENUS	*Pogona* (formerly *Amphibolurus*)	7 species of ground and tree lizards of Australia
SPECIES	*Pogona vitticeps*	bearded dragon

You may have heard lizards called "herps." Reptiles and amphibians—frogs, toads, salamanders, and newts—together are called herptiles. This word comes from the Greek word *herpeton,* meaning "creeping thing." The study of reptiles and amphibians is called *herpetology (her-*puh-*tahl-*uh-jee), and people who own "herps" are called "herpers."

I didn't decide to get the bearded dragon right away. I wanted to do some reading first. I checked out lizard books from the library to learn more.

Wild bearded dragons come from Australia, and they live in a lot of different environments. They live in woodlands that are warm and rainy, or savannahs or deserts, which are hotter and drier. They spend most of their time perched on logs, rocks, fence posts, bushes, and tree trunks or low branches. They live close to the ground.

An adult bearded dragon has spiny scales covering its throat.

Bearded dragons are calm, gentle, and basically friendly. They are interested in people.

Baby bearded dragons hatch from eggs, like chickens. When bearded dragons hatch, they are 4 or 5 inches long. They grow all their lives, and they can grow to be 16 to 22 inches long. But their skin doesn't grow with them, so they shed it. Shedding skin is called molting. Bearded dragons molt a little bit at a time, in patches.

Bearded dragons are one of the best lizards for a first-time lizard owner. They are easy to take care of and handle. They can be happy and healthy in a cage. They are very tame, and they have friendly personalities. Also, they are fun to watch.

Tyson is good at handling lizards. He showed me a leopard gecko and a baby savannah monitor, too.

After I read about bearded dragons, my dad and I went back to the store. I held the baby bearded, and it didn't get scared. Tyson, who works at the store with my dad, showed me some other lizards.

When you are trying to decide what kind of lizard to get, you have to ask some questions. How big will the lizard get? What kind of diet does it need? Is it gentle? You don't want a lizard that will attack or bite. You also have to think about the lizard's habits, like if it is active during the day or night. And you have to know what kind of habitat, or environment, it needs.

You can buy lizards at many pet stores. Some stores sell just reptiles—lizards, snakes, and turtles. And you can buy lizards from people who breed them. They mate the lizards and raise babies to sell. You can also buy lizards through the Internet or by mail order. But then you wouldn't get to see or hold the pet before you got it.

After I thought about all the different lizards, I decided to get the bearded dragon. He was cool looking and friendly. We looked him over to make sure he was healthy. He seemed alert, with his eyes wide open. His mouth, eyes, and feet were in good condition. His skin didn't have any cuts or scars. He was a little chubby, but not fat.

A special thing to do when you buy a lizard is to count all its toes. Baby lizards will nip at each other's toes and sometimes bite them off.

I put my lizard in a box to take it home, so it wouldn't get scared or run away.

At the same time, we bought the equipment we would need: an aquarium, a screen for the top, a heating pad, a special light, plastic turf for the bottom of the tank, a thermometer, and some vitamins. We also bought crickets for food. The bearded dragon cost about $80, and the equipment was $75. My dad and I each paid half. I earned my money by helping with chores around the house. Also, my grandma gives me $20 for every A I get at school! Last year I got all A's.

I've had the bearded dragon for about a year. I named him Eggie. He has grown to about 12 inches. A couple of months ago, I bought a new bearded dragon, a female.

I got the female as an adult. So far I haven't thought of a name for her. I think whoever owned her before me did not treat her very well. At first she wasn't nice. She didn't like to be touched and she didn't like Eggie. But I kept petting her and petting her, so she got used to me. Now she is nice to me. And she and Eggie get along fine.

It takes a while for lizards to become friends.

Lizards must have heat and light...

A kid's bedroom isn't exactly a lizard's natural habitat. But you can keep a lizard healthy if you have the right cage.

I've learned a lot by having a lizard, especially about habitats. You can't just put a lizard into any old cage. If you do, the lizard might get sick or die. You have to do research to find out what kind of habitat your lizard needs.

I keep my two bearded dragons in an aquarium. It's a 20-gallon tank, which is okay because they are still small. When they get bigger, they will need more room. Some people buy a 40- or 50-gallon tank to start with.

The bearded dragons are in a cage that is more wide than tall, because in the wild they live close to the ground. But the chameleons' tank is taller. Wild chameleons live in trees. Our chameleons' cage gives them room to climb. The chameleons' cage also has a lot more plants than the dragons' cage.

My bearded dragons might grow another 6 to 12 inches. I've started saving money for a bigger cage.

Basking means lying in the sun, or under a light, and getting warm.

The most important part of keeping a lizard is lighting and heating the cage. Lizards *must* have heat and light. Ultraviolet light, like sunlight, makes them hungry. It also helps them digest food and stay healthy. Lizards must have heat because they are cold-blooded. This means they get their body heat from their surroundings.

People are warm-blooded. Our bodies stay pretty much the same temperature no matter what the weather is like. But lizards have to bask in the sun to get warm. If they get too hot, they move into the shade.

For the bearded dragons, I keep the temperature in the aquarium at 80°F (27°C) during the day. If it's colder than that all day, they will get sick. But the temperature shouldn't go over 90°F (32°C) because that's too hot. The chameleon tank is a little warmer. To keep the cages the right temperature, I put a heating pad underneath the turf on the bottom of each cage.

Different kinds of lizards need different climates. I have a thermometer in each of my tanks so I know how warm they are.

Lizards like to bask from branches at different levels in the cage. You might need another kind of aquarium heater to keep the all-over temperature high.

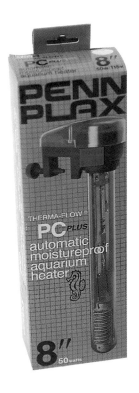

Other ways to heat a lizard cage are with heater bulbs, ceramic heaters, and rocks that heat up. These "hot rocks" really don't work very well, though. A lizard feels heat only when it comes from above, the way sunlight does. A lizard sitting on a hot rock might not notice if it gets too hot and burns its belly. Some people who raise lizards say you should never use a hot rock with a bearded dragon.

Off to one side at the top of my lizards' cages, I shine a spotlight on a rock or branch. This light is hot, about 88° to 95°F (31° to 35°C). It lets the lizards bask in the heat, the way they do in the wild. The spotlight is an ordinary lightbulb, except it is wider.

To give my lizards "sunlight," I put a long fluorescent lightbulb at the top of their cage. It's called a full-spectrum fluorescent bulb. This light doesn't give off heat, but it gives off ultraviolet (UV) light, the same as sunlight.

In the wild, lizards are used to being colder at night. I shut off the heating pads and the lights at night. The temperature in the cages drops to the temperature of my bedroom. Like people, bearded dragons and chameleons are active during the day. This works out well, because my lizards sleep while I'm sleeping at night.

The UV light rays from fluorescent bulbs help lizards make vitamin D in their bodies. They need this vitamin to grow bones and stay healthy.

Lizards drink the water you spray in their cages. Some lizards will drink from water dishes, too.

All lizards need fresh air in their cage. You have to make sure they get plenty of air through the wire screen that covers the top of the cage. Some lizard cages are built of wood. There are holes in the sides for air to come through.

Another important part of a lizard's habitat is humidity—how much water is in the air. I spray the bearded dragon tank with water every couple of days. The chameleons need more humidity, so we spray their tank twice a day.

It's fun to decide what else to put inside your lizards' cage. First, you have to have something covering the bottom of the cage and the heating pad. This covering is called the substrate. It can be taken out and cleaned or replaced. If you don't have any substrate, germs from the lizards' poops build up, and the lizards might get sick. For substrate, we use plastic grass turf. It's easy to wash and keep clean. You can also use newspaper or paper towels. Don't use gravel for bearded dragons, because they might eat it! It's hard to clean, too.

You can buy bark, cloth, or plastic turf to use for substrate. I like turf, because it lifts right out when I clean the cage.

Creating a Natural Habitat

The equipment you choose for your lizard will depend on the species you choose. It will also depend on the temperature of the room where you keep the cage, and whether the cage is in a bright or dark spot.

Savannah or Desert

Design this habitat for a desert iguana, or other lizards that come from areas that are warm and dry. For the **substrate,** use gravel, plastic turf, or newspaper. In the substrate, place granite and limestone **rocks** or tufa rock, and **wood** such as driftwood. For **heating** and **lighting,** you may need a spotlight, ceramic heater, heating pad, or fluorescent light. For **plants,** try a cactus that isn't too spiny, or an aloe or yucca. Put a small ceramic **water** bowl in the cage. Spray the cage with water in the evening.

Woodland or Forest

Create this habitat for a tokay gecko, or other ground or tree species from temperate (mild) and tropical regions. For **substrate**, use chipped bark, plastic turf, or sterile peat moss. Place **rocks** and **wood** in the substrate. For **heating** and **lighting** use a full-spectrum fluorescent tube light and a heating pad. Many types of **plants** will grow well in this environment, including ivy and ferns. Mist the cage daily with **water.**

Tall Forest

This habitat is designed for tree-living species, such as chameleons and some geckos. The aquarium or cage should be taller than it is wide. For **substrate,** use bark chips, plastic turf, or sterile peat moss. **Rocks** and **branches** can be placed in the substrate. Design the **heating** and **lighting** as you would for a forest habitat. Grow **plants** to keep the humidity high. Try Spanish moss, pothos, dragon tree, hibiscus, or ornamental fig.

Lizards need a place to do their basking. A branch or piece of driftwood works well. I have pieces of driftwood in the beardeds' cage. You can also use a large, flat rock. I have been looking by the creek for a rock for my beardeds. Lizards also like logs or hollow branches, because these are places to hide. A while ago, I got some plastic plants for my beardeds' cage. They seem happier since I got the plants.

My dad carved my driftwood into the shape of lizards. It's cool, because you have to look at the pieces of wood for a minute before you realize they are lizards.

Chameleons like to climb and explore. You have to watch them!

The chameleons have a different setup. We put lots of branches and taller plants in their tank. It's like a mini rain forest. They climb all around.

Once, one of our chameleons escaped. She climbed to the very top of the highest branch in the cage and crawled out through the opening for the lightbulb cord. She climbed up the curtains and up on top of the curtain rod. My brother and I tried to get her down, but we couldn't reach her. Finally my dad came in and returned the adventurer to her cage.

Taking care of lizards is easy...

Once you have the cage set up, it's easy to take care of lizards. I think they're one of the easiest pets—less work than cats, dogs, or fish.

Bearded dragons are omnivores. That means they eat both plants and animals. I feed the bearded dragons crickets, mealworms, pinkies, and vegetables. Do you know what a pinkie is? It's not your little finger! It's a newborn mouse. Newborn mice don't have any hair yet, so they're all pink. When we buy pinkies, they are already dead. They come frozen, so you have to thaw them out before you feed them to your lizards.

If you don't like the idea of feeding live food to your pet, then lizards aren't the pet for you.

I feed my lizards as much as they can eat in 5 minutes. Crickets that aren't eaten will jump around and annoy the lizards.

When Eggie was young, I fed him every day. Now I only feed him and the girl dragon every other day. They get about 10 crickets at a time, and a few mealworms. They seem to like the pinkies best, but I only give them one once a week. Mice have a lot of fat in them. Eating too many would be bad for the lizards. They could get fat or have health problems, just like people who eat too many french fries or potato chips.

I breed the crickets myself. They live in a little plastic box, a mini aquarium. On the bottom of the cage, I put some straw and a water bowl. I also give them cardboard toilet paper rolls, so they have places to rest and hide. Crickets eat pretty much anything. I mainly give my crickets fish food. You start out with just a few crickets, and pretty soon you have a ton of them.

Before I give the crickets to my lizards, I feed the crickets. This is called "gut loading." You make sure the crickets are full of food so that when the lizards eat the crickets, they'll be getting an extra-healthy meal.

Adult bearded dragons sit still and wait for the crickets to get close to them. Younger bearded dragons will chase the crickets.

To feed my lizards their vitamins, I sprinkle vegetables or crickets with the powder. Lizards seem to like powder-covered food as much as plain food.

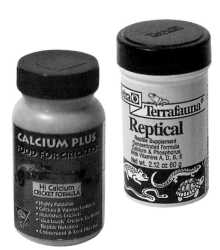

I also feed my bearded dragons vegetables. In the wild, bearded dragons eat some plants. My beardeds like greens, such as lettuce, and soft vegetables, like peas and corn. They also eat carrot peels, green beans, and other kinds of beans. They like little pieces of oranges, apples, and bananas, too.

I give my lizards extra vitamins and minerals twice a week. We buy a powder at the pet store. The one I use has calcium and vitamin D in it. Once in a while I give them other vitamins. You just have to be careful to not give lizards too much vitamin A. It makes them sick.

Lizard Food

In the wild, **bearded dragons** will eat worms, insects, and plants, especially fruits and flowers. Here are some ideas for foods to give your bearded dragon:

Insects *(about 60% of diet)*
- crickets
- grasshoppers
- mealworms
- earthworms

Greens *(about 40% of diet)*
- turnip greens
- collard greens
- mustard greens
- spinach
- kale
- chard
- chicory
- escarole
- Boston lettuce (not iceberg)

Other Vegetables & Fruits
(occasionally, in small pieces)
- grated carrots
- tomatoes
- cucumbers
- squash
- apples
- pears
- bananas
- grapes
- oranges
- cooked potatoes
- peas
- beans
- strawberries
- melon

Chameleons eat mainly insects, but they will be healthiest if they eat a variety of foods. At every feeding, offer chameleons a few small pieces of fresh fruits and vegetables. Avoid spinach, lettuce, and cabbage. Here are a few ideas:

- collard greens
- mustard greens
- turnip greens

- sugar snap pea pods
- bean sprouts
- sliced apples

You have to keep an eye on any lizard that's out of its cage. My bearded dragons keep an eye on me, too.

I clean my lizards' cages once a week. It's actually kind of fun. Here is how I do it. First I take all the stuff out of the tanks, one tank at a time— the driftwood, plants, turf, heating pad, and, of course, the lizards. While I'm cleaning the bearded dragons' cage, sometimes I just put them on my shoulders. They stay there the whole time. Or I ask my brother or sister to watch them for a while. Chameleons have to be watched more carefully when they're out of the cage.

Next I take the turf into the bathroom. I dump everything on it into the toilet. Usually there's some dead skin and some poops. The poops are kind of wet, but not too messy. Then I wash the turf in warm water. Sometimes I wash the plastic plants and the driftwood, too. I hang the turf up to dry.

In the summer, I spray the turf with a hose outside. When the weather isn't good, I clean the turf in the bathtub.

It's a good idea to wash your hands after you handle your lizards, especially after you clean their cage.

I clean the bottoms and sides of the cages with a rag and warm water. Sometimes I use dish soap and rinse the cages really well with water. Finally, I put everything back in place. The last thing I do is spray water on the walls.

That's it. It doesn't take long. You'd have to be pretty lazy to say that taking care of lizards is hard!

Eggie doesn't like to be ignored...

When I get older, I want to be a vet or a doctor. I know for sure I will have a lot of pets. Even now, I'm not that crazy about toys—I'd rather play with my animals. I spend about an hour or two every day with my pets, taking care of them and playing with them.

Eggie likes to play and be petted. Mostly, he doesn't like to be ignored. He doesn't mind if I flip him over in my hand and rub his belly. He also likes water. He loves to float in a sink or tub with a little warm water.

Lizards don't need baths. But some lizards like to soak in shallow, warm water. Soaking is good for them, too.

A male and female bearded dragon can live together, or two females. But two males in the same cage will fight.

The female bearded dragon isn't as nice. She's fussy. She hates water. And when she gets mad, her beard pops out and she bobs her head up and down. When I first got her, she didn't like Eggie. She blew up her beard and hissed. But I kept putting them together and petting them, and they started to like each other. They are pals now. They lie on top of each other when they sleep.

Part of having a pet is keeping your pet safe. Sometimes you have to make rules.

It's easy to handle bearded dragons. You just pick them up under the belly and hold them in your palm. Of course, my beardeds also climb on my shoulders and arms and head, like I'm a tree.

It's important to treat lizards nicely. You have to be gentle. One time some of my friends came over and were too rough with Eggie. It made me mad. After that I put up a sign on my bedroom door that says "Do not touch animals or hurt them."

If a bearded dragon doesn't flare out its beard much, that's a good thing. That means the lizard feels comfortable and safe.

You can tell if bearded dragons are afraid of something. If they're scared or don't want to be held, they'll jump off you and start running. They can run pretty fast. They also flatten their bodies when they're upset. If they're really scared or mad, they will puff out their beards. Sometimes my female dragon bites me. Actually, she just sort of gums me. It feels gooey.

Most of the time, the bearded dragons either just sit around, or they hide under the pieces of wood and go in the corners of the cage. The other thing they do a lot is bask in the heat light.

If your lizards' cages are set up right, the lizards will probably stay healthy. Sometimes if you get a new lizard, especially if it was wild, it could have a disease. Lizards that come from the wild can have ticks, mites, or worms. You can stop diseases from spreading by keeping a new lizard in a separate cage for a few weeks, to make sure it's not sick.

Your lizards can get sick if you feed them the wrong foods, or if you don't keep their cage clean, or if the cage is too cold or too hot. A bad diet can give lizards diarrhea, which is serious for them. Sometimes lizards get skin infections or injuries. Lizards can also get colds.

Stress is one of the main reasons lizards get sick. Some lizards get stressed when they're handled too much, but most bearded dragons like careful handling.

Molting

Lizard skin is strange stuff. It may be horny or scaly. It can look like beads or pebbles or grains. Lizard skin is strange in another way. It is not alive, so it doesn't grow.

Your skin grows, so as your body grows bigger, your skin still fits. But a lizard's skin no longer fits as the lizard grows. The too-small skin must be shed from time to time. Underneath the old skin is new skin that fits. This shedding is called molting.

Lizards molt in different ways. Some slip out of their old skins, the way snakes do. They leave the old skin behind in one piece. Other lizards, such as bearded dragons, lose their skin in patches or shreds. You will probably see little pieces of skin in the cage.

Geckos might be the strangest molters of all. They grasp their old skin in their mouth, pull it from their body, and eat it!

43

A lizard won't tell you when something is wrong. You have to know your pet's behavior and notice things yourself.

With any pet, if you spend a lot of time with it, you can usually tell if something's wrong. You know how it normally acts, so you will notice if there's a change. If the lizard isn't eating as much as it usually does, that might be a sign that it's sick. If its poops look different from usual, that's another sign. Or the lizard's skin might look strange, or you could see a cut. If you notice anything that seems different about your lizard, you should probably take it to a veterinarian.

So far, I've never had to bring my lizards to the vet. They are healthy. I think they're pretty happy, too.

Chameleons have many moods...

My chameleon turns blue when I put her on a blue chair.

Everyone knows that chameleons can change colors. Our chameleons are usually green, but they also turn brown, blue, and black. Other kinds of chameleons turn brown, tan, red, orange, and as bright yellow as a lemon.

Not everyone knows that chameleons are a type of lizard—the *chamaeleonidae*. In books, chameleons are sometimes called chameleonids. Whatever you call them, chameleons are like other lizards in some ways. In other ways, they are not like any other lizard.

Chameleons are famous for changing colors. But some other lizards can change colors, too, like this gecko (below), blending into a tree.

In the wild, chameleons change color to blend in with things around them, so snakes and birds cannot find them and eat them. Chameleons also blend into things by the way they move and use their body. A chameleon can flatten its body and move like a leaf blowing on a tree. Or it might turn brown and stay still like a stick or a chip of wood. Some chameleons' skin looks just like moss!

Most people think that chameleons change color just to match what's around them. But there's a lot more to it than that. There are other things that make a chameleon change color, like light, temperature, how healthy it is, whether it's scared or angry, and if it is mating.

You can tell that chameleons are active in the daytime because they have round pupils in their eyes. Reptiles that are active at night have pupils shaped like slits. You can tell chameleons are climbers by looking at their toes and tail.

Chameleons' tails can curl around branches and twigs and hold them. Chameleons have really, really long, sticky tongues. They are the champion insect-eaters. Their tongues dart out faster than a bug can fly. Their eyes are amazing, too. One eye can look forward while the other one looks backward! Chameleons' toes can grip tree branches and bushes. Chameleons are very good climbers.

At our house, we have veiled chameleons *(Chamaeleo calyptratus).* They originally come from the mountains of Yemen and Saudi Arabia, countries in the Middle East. The climate there is tropical to subtropical, so we keep our chameleons' cage warm. We keep the air moist by spraying the walls of the cage and the plants with water twice a day. This is how the chameleons get all their drinking water. They won't drink from a bowl.

Some books I've read say you should use an all-screen cage for chameleons. They get more fresh air in an all-screen cage. But then it's harder to keep the cage humid.

Spraying chameleons lets them drink the way they would in the wild. They lap up water droplets from leaves.

Besides the light in their cage, chameleons also need real sunlight. Their cage is in the sun for part of the day. In the summer, my dad takes them outside. I watch them so they don't run away. But usually they stay on a tree or a plant.

We also put the chameleons on our plants in the house. They really like this big tree we have in the living room. They stay there for 4 or 5 or even 10 hours.

The best kinds of plants for a chameleon cage are pothos and hibiscus. Whatever plants you use, be sure they aren't poisonous.

Different Kinds of Chameleons

3-Horned Chameleon

There are about 100 species of chameleons. You won't find most of them in a pet store, but sometimes wild chameleons are caught and sold to pet stores. Many are sick, because they haven't been well cared for on their way to the store. This problem is getting better, because new laws make it harder to sell wild chameleons. Just the same, you need to choose a chameleon carefully.

Only a few species have been bred for life in a cage.

Good chameleons to start with include the veiled chameleon (*Chamaeleo calyptratus*), Jackson's chameleon (*Chamaeleo jacksonii*), and the panther chameleon (*Chamaeleo pardalis*). Veiled and panther chameleons like warm temperatures (80° to 90°F during the day), and Jackson's prefer a cooler climate (mid-70s daytime). They all do best with a 10-15 degree temperature drop at night.

Lizards called anoles (uh-*noh*-leez) are sometimes sold in pet stores as "chameleons." Anoles change color, too, but they are not chameleons. They need different care.

Parson's Chameleon (male)

Panther Chameleon (female)

Jewel Chameleon (female)

Balteatus Chameleon (female)

Chameleons like real plants better than plastic ones. You can grow live plants in potting soil in the cage, but it makes it harder to keep the cage clean. The chameleons' droppings fall in the dirt, and dirt is harder to clean than turf. That's why we have plastic plants in our cage.

We feed our chameleons a handful of crickets or mealworms every other day—crickets more often than mealworms. Sometimes I catch a bug outside, a locust or a moth, and give it to the chameleons. That's a special treat for them. We also give them extra vitamins and minerals.

A chameleon can use its long tongue to catch a cricket on the other side of the cage. Chameleons' tongues are almost as long as their bodies!

My dad sometimes holds the chameleons on a stick. He lets them climb onto it themselves. That way he can take them from their cage without handling them too much.

One big difference between bearded dragons and chameleons is that you can't touch or handle chameleons much. If you handle them a lot, they could die from stress. I can tell they're stressed out when their beards turn yellow. If you do hold them, you have to be very careful. Hold them gently with your fingers around the middle of the body. You should never grab a chameleon by the neck or backbone. That makes them scared. In our house, usually only our dad is allowed to take the chameleons out and hold them.

Color isn't the only way to know a chameleon's mood. To really learn about chameleons, you have to watch them a lot.

Most chameleons like to be alone. They get stressed out when they are around other chameleons. Veiled chameleons can live with each other, but you can't have more than one male. Two males will fight. We have two females and one male.

Chameleons have many different moods. Sometimes they're excited and they move around. Sometimes they're calm. Other times they feel lousy and they just sit there. If a chameleon is mad, it might turn a dark color and open its mouth. If it's really mad, it swings its tail.

If a chameleon turns pale white, yellow, or green and its mouth is hanging open, that means it's overheated. You have to cool it down right away. If it closes its eyes for a really long time, it might be sick. If the chameleon is a bright color but its eyes look sunken, it's thirsty and needs water.

Chameleons are trickier to keep as pets than bearded dragons. But I really like chameleons. They move slowly. They look at you and look at you and then they'll move. They walk funny and their eyes move all around. Even though they don't do much, they are still interesting.

The best place to keep your chameleons' cage is someplace quiet. They don't like activity. When we watch our chameleons, we sit very still.

I plan to have lizards for a long time...

A lizard has a personality that might or might not match your own.

I'm glad I decided to get lizards. They're great pets. They are easy to take care of, and they are clean and quiet. They don't smell bad or take up a lot of space. I love to watch them, and I've learned a lot. Still, lizards are not for everyone. If you want a pet to play with a lot, you should probably get a dog or cat.

Amazing Lizards

Cool facts about lizards:

• Some lizards have no legs. They look just like snakes. The only way you can tell them apart is that the lizard has ear openings and moveable eyelids. A snake does not.

• Lizards range in size from 1 inch to 10 feet or longer. The world's largest lizard is the Komodo dragon. It grows to 11 feet. That's as long as a car!

• When some lizards are grabbed by the tail, the tail separates from the lizard's body. The tail continues to wriggle, which confuses the other animal and gives the lizard a chance to escape. The lizard grows another tail, but it is never the same color or length as the original. If your lizard is able to drop its tail, you must handle the lizard extra carefully.

• Reptiles continue to grow throughout their lives.

• Many lizards have moveable ribs, which allow them to flatten their body.

• Geckos have a number of overlapping flaps under their toes. These flaps, called lamellae (luh-*meh*-lee), are covered with tiny, backward-pointing hooks. They allow geckos to hold on to any surface. A gecko can climb a glass window or hang from the ceiling.

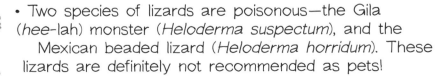

• Two species of lizards are poisonous—the Gila (*hee*-lah) monster (*Heloderma suspectum*), and the Mexican beaded lizard (*Heloderma horridum*). These lizards are definitely not recommended as pets!

My bearded dragons could be with me for a long time. They live 4 to 10 years. Male chameleons live 4 to 8 years. But female chameleons have a shorter life span. They only live 2 to 3 years. Maybe I'll take my bearded dragons with me when I go to college.

I like my "beardies" so much that I decided to start breeding them. That's why I got the female, as a mate for Eggie. I had to do some reading to find out how to get lizards to mate.

To breed lizards, you have to be sure you have a male and a female. It's kind of hard to tell them apart. With bearded dragons, males usually have wider heads and thicker tails.

At first the eggs were white. After a while, they turned orange.

It's not an automatic thing, like love at first sight. Lizards know that it's time to mate by changes in weather and season. It's like they say, "Oh, it's spring! Let's have some babies." What happens is that their bodies notice the warmer temperature and longer daylight hours.

When you keep lizards in a cage, you have to try to make them think the season has changed. What I did was start keeping the cage a little warmer. I raised the temperature little by little every couple of days until it reached about 92°F (33°C). I also left the light on longer.

When the female was ready to mate, she lifted her leg. Eggie climbed on top of her. I couldn't really see exactly what was going on. About two weeks later, the female laid eggs. I moved the eggs into a plastic box filled with sand.

I kept the temperature in the plastic box at 84°F (29°C). I was excited! The eggs looked like little rocks—actually, more like rock candy but kind of speckled. I kept the cage moist by spraying water in it every couple of days. I just had to wait for the eggs to hatch. I read that it would take 55 to 75 days, so I would have to be patient.

Lizards don't sit on their nests or take care of their eggs. They just leave the eggs to hatch by themselves.

If you learn how to take care of a lizard, a lizard is a good pet and a friend.

I waited more than 75 days, but the eggs never hatched! I felt very bad. I asked my dad what happened. He thought that the temperature wasn't quite high enough, or that the eggs were infertile— unable to grow. I was really disappointed.

I'm going to try again. I want to learn how to breed lizards so I can have more of them. I plan to have lizards for a long time.

Glossary

Bask: to warm by lying in the sun or under a bright light

Chameleon (kuh-*mee*-lee-uhn): a type of lizard that can change colors, has a tail that can grasp, and has eyes that move in any direction

Desert: an area of land that cannot support most life because it is too hot and dry. Many wild lizards live in deserts.

Diarrhea (dye-uh-*ree*-uh): a condition in which an animal has runny stools (poops). Diarrhea is a sign of an unhealthy diet or an illness.

Habitat: the place where a plant or animal normally lives

Herp: short for herptile, a reptile or amphibian

Herpetology (her-puh-*tahl*-uh-jee): the study of reptiles and amphibians

Humidity (hyoo-*mid*-uh-tee): the amount of water in the air

Gecko: a small lizard that makes loud calling sounds. Many geckos are expert climbers.

Gut loading: feeding insects before feeding the insects to a lizard

Iguana (ih-*gwah*-nah): a large American lizard that eats plants

Molt: to shed skin, fur, or feathers. When snakes or lizards molt, they shed their skin.

Monitor (*mahn*-uh-tur): a lizard with strong legs and a powerful tail. Monitors can grow to be very large.

Omnivore (*ahm*-nih-vor): an animal that eats both plants and animals

Reptile: an animal that crawls on its belly or on short legs, and has scales or bony plates on its body. Reptiles include alligators, crocodiles, lizards, snakes, turtles, tortoises, and the tuatara.

Savannah: a usually dry area in which mainly grasses grow, and a few trees. Many animals live on savannahs, including some lizards.

Species (*spee*-sheez): a group of animals or plants that are basically alike

Substrate: the material covering the bottom of a cage

Temperate: neither very hot nor very cold

Terrarium: a container for growing plants or keeping small animals

Tropical: describes a warm, moist area in which plants can grow year-round

Vivarium: a cage for reptiles

Resources

American Animal Hospital Association (AAHA)
P.O. Box 150899
Denver, CO 80215
(303) 986-2800
veterinarian referral line: (800) 883-6301
www.healthypet.com
An international organization of more than 17,000 veterinary care providers. Call or write for a free pamphlet on pet health care.

American Federation of Herpetoculturists/ *The Vivarium* magazine
P. O. Box 300067
Escondido, CA 92030-0067
(760) 747-4948

American Veterinary Medical Association
Public Information Division
1931 North Meacham Road, Suite 100
Schaumburg, IL 60173-4360
(847) 925-8070
www.avma.org
Brochures are available from the AVMA on selecting a pet, sterilization, choosing a veterinarian, and careers in veterinary science. The AVMA has also developed a classroom program for fourth graders called "People and Animals Sharing the World," to help students better understand the role of animals in human society.

The Animal Network
htt043://animalnetwork.com
Check out the "Reptile Roundup" for information on your favorite lizard.

Association of Reptile and Amphibian Veterinarians (ARAV)
Wilbur Armand, Executive Director
6 North Pennel Rd.
Media, PA 19063
(610) 358-9530
Call this office to find a vet in your area who is a member of ARAV.

Chameleon Conservation Society
http://orsp1.adm.binghamton.edu/~steve/CCS/

***Reptile & Amphibian* magazine**
1168 Route 61 Hiway South
Pottsville, PA 17901

***Reptiles* magazine**
P. O. Box 58700
Boulder, CO 80322-8700
(800) 365-4421

For a look at more of the latest Web sites devoted to herps or reptiles, do your own search. You may want to narrow your search by keeping to one particular type of lizard, such as "iguanas," "geckos," or "chameleons."

Most large cities have a herpetological society. Check your phone book to find a herpers group near you.

For Further Reading

Arnold, Caroline. *Watching Desert Wildlife*. Photographs by
Arthur Arnold. Minneapolis: Carolrhoda, 1997.

Coborn, John. *The Proper Care of Reptiles*. Neptune City, NJ:
TFH Publications, 1993.

de Vosjoli, Philippe and Robert Malloux. *The General Care and
Maintenance of Bearded Dragons*. Lakeside, CA: Advanced
Vivarium Systems, Inc., 1993.

de Vosjoli, Philippe and Gary Ferguson, ed. *Care and Breeding of
Panther, Jackson's, Veiled and Parson's Chameleons*. Santee,
CA: Advanced Vivarium Systems, Inc., 1995.

Jes, Harald. *Lizards in the Terrarium*. Hauppauge, NY: Barron's
Educational Series, 1987.

LeBerre, Francois. *The New Chameleon Handbook: Everything
About Selection, Care, Diet, Disease, Reproduction, and
Behavior*. Hauppauge, NY: Barron's Educational Series, 1995.

Schnieper, Claudia. *Chameleons*. Photographs by Max Meier.
Minneapolis: Carolrhoda, 1991.

Schnieper, Claudia. *Lizards*. Photographs by Max Meier.
Minneapolis: Carolrhoda, 1990.

Snedden, Robert. *What Is a Reptile?* San Francisco: Sierra Club
Books for Children, 1994.

Souza, D. M. *Catch Me If You Can: A Book About Lizards*.
Minneapolis: Carolrhoda, 1992.

Staniszewski, Marc. *The Manual of Lizards and Snakes. A
Salamander Book*. Morris Plains, NJ: Tetra Press, 1990.

Index

activity, 14, 23, 46
anoles, 49
attention, lizards' need for, 17, 34, 37, 43

babies, 10, 13, 15
basking, 20, 22, 27, 40
beards, 10, 12, 38, 40, 51
behavior changes, 43
biting, 9, 14, 15, 40
breeding bearded dragons, 56–59

cages, cleaning, 25, 34–36, 50; location of 26, 53; setting up 21–28; size of, 18–19; types of, 18–19, 24, 26, 47
chameleon species, 47, 49
choosing a lizard, 14–15
classification, scientific, 11
cleanliness, 36, 37, 54
climbing ability, of chameleons, 28, 46; of geckos, 55
coloring, of bearded dragons, 10; of chameleons, 44–45, 51–52
compatibility, of lizards, 38, 52
crickets, breeding, 31

diarrhea, 41
diet, 14, 29–33, 41, 50
diseases. See illness.
droppings, 25, 35, 43, 50

ears, 55
eggs, 13, 57–59
environments, 12, 14. See also habitats.
equipment, 16, 26. See also cages.
eyes, 15, 46, 53, 55

fear, signs of in lizards, 40, 45
fighting, 38, 52
friendliness, 9, 13, 17

geckos, 11, 14, 26, 42, 45, 55
gut loading, 31

habitats, 14, 18, 24, 26, 47. See also environments.
handling lizards, 39, 41, 51, 55
health, signs of in lizards, 15, 45
heating a cage, 20–23, 26, 49, 57
herptiles, 11
humidity, 24, 26, 47

iguanas, 26
illness, 18, 25, 32, 41, 43, 52

life span, 56
lighting a cage, 20, 22–23, 26, 48, 57

mating, 15, 45, 56–57
molting, 13, 42
monitors, 14
moods, of chameleons, 45, 52

names, scientific, 11

pet stores, 15, 32, 49
plants, 19, 26, 27–28, 48, 50
poisonous lizards, 55

reptiles, 15, 46, 55

size, 10, 13, 14, 17, 19, 55
skin, 9, 10, 13, 15, 41, 42, 43
sleeping, 23
species, defined, 11
stress, 41, 51–52
substrate, 25, 26
sunlight, 22–23, 48

tails, 46, 52, 55
tongues, chameleon, 46, 50

veterinarians, when to visit, 43
vitamins and minerals, 23, 32, 50

water, 24, 26, 24, 26, 47, 58
wild, lizards in, 12, 19, 23, 32, 33, 41, 45

ABOUT THE AUTHOR

LeeAnne Engfer is a writer and editor. She graduated from the University of Minnesota with degrees in journalism and French. Her interests include animals, books, cooking, travel, and yoga. She lives in St. Paul, Minnesota, with her husband, David, and their three cats.

ABOUT THE PHOTOGRAPHER

Andy King is a native of Boulder, Colorado, and a graduate of Colorado State University. Andy has traveled around the world as a documentary and corporate photographer, and he has worked as a photographer at newspapers in Minnesota and Texas. He lives with his wife, Patricia, and their daughter in St. Paul, Minnesota, where he enjoys mountain biking and playing basketball.